An Allowable Deduction:
The Ultimate Book of Accounting Cartoons

Featuring Cartoons From
Barron's
The New Yorker
The Wall Street Journal
and more!

Front Cover illustration: Leo Cullum
Back Cover illustration: P.C. Vey
Introduction: Bob Mankoff
Edited By: Darren Kornblut

Dedicated to Jennifer, Bea, and Steven Zelin (the Singing CPA)

Cartoon Collections, LLC
10 Grand Central, 29th Floor
New York, NY 10017

For cartoon licensing information visit www.cartoonstock.com
Create a personlized version of this book at www.cartoonstockgifts.com

First edition published 2024

Item # 49189
ISBN: 978-1-963079-11-1

Introduction

Hi, Bob Mankoff, former cartoon editor of *The New Yorker*, here to welcome you to the wonderful world of accounting cartoons! I've culled the best of them from CartoonStock.com to give you a lighthearted look at the profession that enables businesses to thrive and embezzlers to be put in jail.

Accountants play an essential role in a market economy by providing accurate and reliable information we often choose to ignore. Not their fault.

But if it makes us feel better to poke fun at them, they should tolerate the ribbing at least, as well as lawyers who not only take our cartoons in stride but pass them around.

From the daily struggles reconciling bank statements to the joys of tax evasion, the cartoons in this book capture the absurd aspects of a profession of control freaks confronted by clients who have receipts in shoeboxes.

Whether you are an accountant or enjoy a good laugh, I'm sure you will find something in these cartoons that is both funny and true. So sit back and let the laughs flow into the funny column of the ledger.

"When you're nailing the numbers, they don't ask questions."

"Happy fiscal year to you, too!"

MEET SANTA'S ENTOURAGE

Larry B - his accountant
"Looks like he's going to have a mighty good year!"

Marge Z - his lawyer
"I love him like a son."

Barney G - his agent and P.R. man
"I'm sorry, but Santa always gets 50% of the gross."

Lorna R - his hairdresser
"Santa's hair is surprisingly fine."

Gerald M - his tailor
"One year, it's buttons, the next year it's no buttons. One year, it's a 5-inch-wide belt, the next year it's gotta be 3½ inches. One year, it's..."

Mrs. Claus - his wife and confidante
"He's really a very sweet man."

r. Chast

3

ACCOUNTING FANTASY CAMP

".... and it was at this point that I realized we made the same mistake as before."

"After state and federal, you get just one wish, and it's half-off chicken wings."

"I realize how helpless and needy they are, but I'm afraid
you still can't claim a human as a dependent."

"And this is our department of experimental accounting."

"It's up to you now, Miller. The only thing that can save us is an accounting breakthrough."

"I'm looking for something accurate but deceivingly hopeful."

"It's so great to be totally away from work that I'm going to move this vacation from the liability column over to assets."

"Mom said I'm her favorite dependent."

"*This is Gondormir, he'll be joining accounting. We're really hoping for some magic.*"

"It's a ransomware attack. Shirley in Accounting is demanding Chardonnay in the vending machines."

"The chart, of course, is nonrepresentational."

"Figures can be misleading – So I've written a song which I think expresses the real story of the firms performance this quarter."

"I never discuss my clients with their mothers."

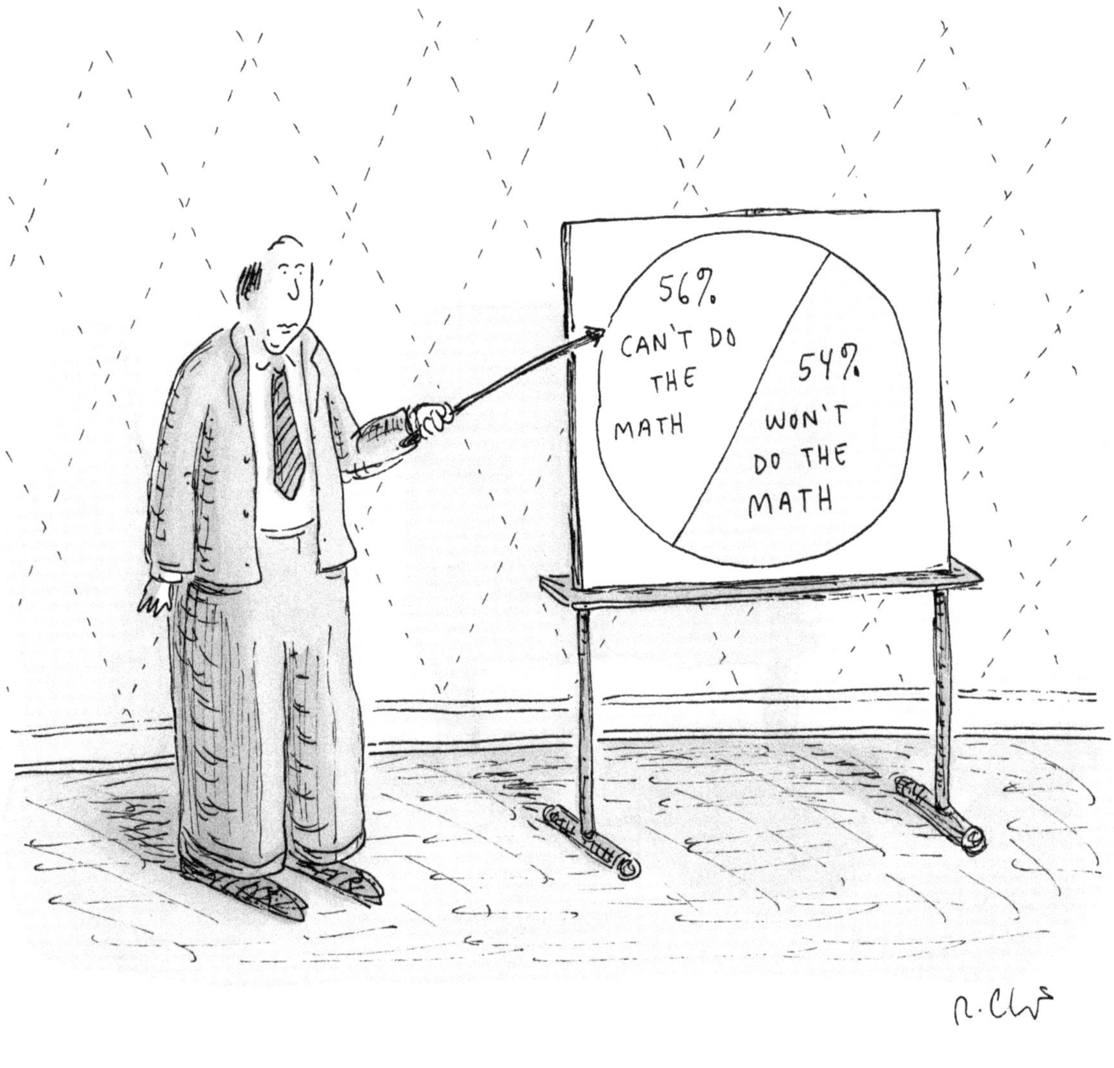
56%
CAN'T DO THE MATH
54%
WON'T DO THE MATH
R. Chast

"*Even if you and your friends do drink to each other's health,*
you can't use your bar tab for a medical expense."

JACK AND THE BEANCOUNTER

PERCIVAL

"We'll make the cow tax deductable."

"It's not enough to write 'Megabucks' on your return, Mr. Clacton. You're supposed to tell us how many."

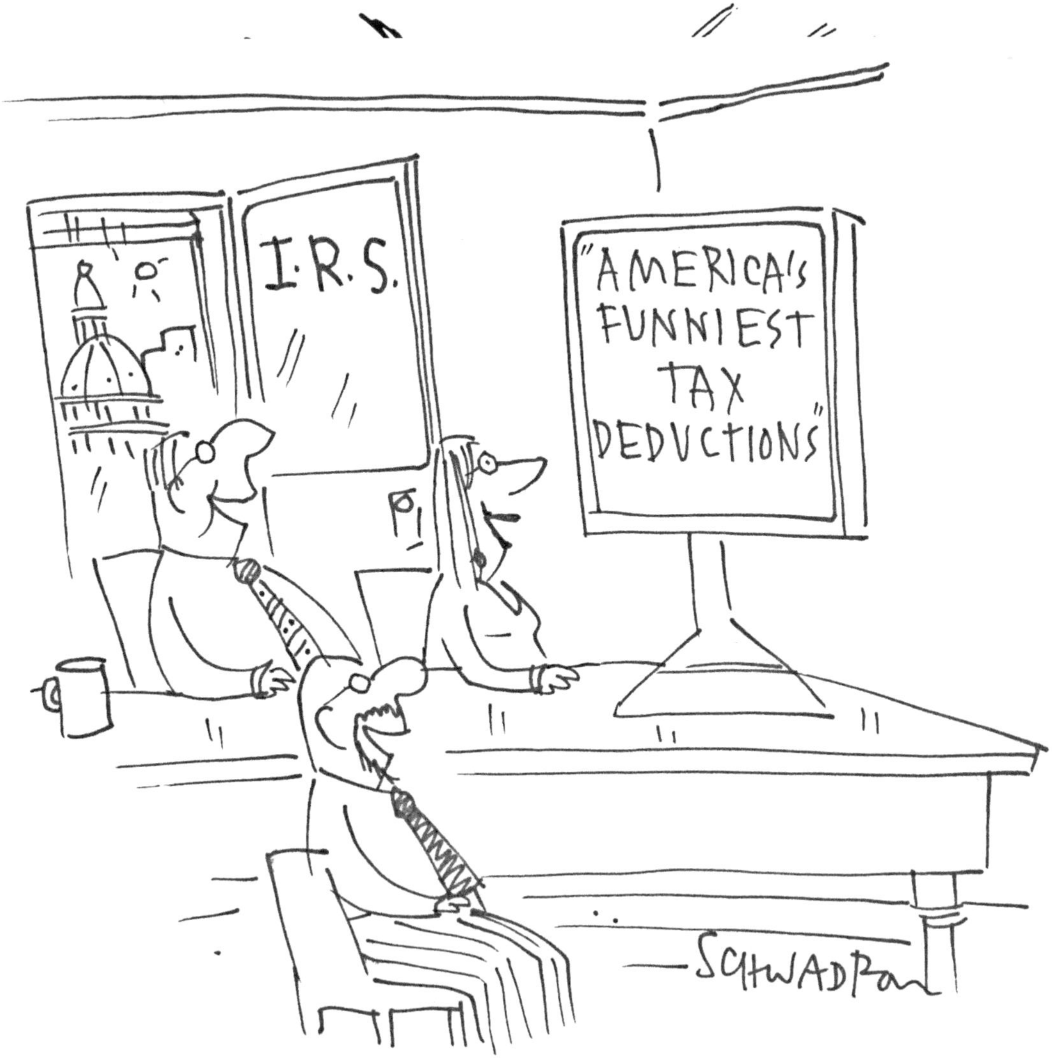
I.R.S.
"AMERICA'S FUNNIEST TAX DEDUCTIONS"
SCHWADRON

"I now pronounce you a joint return."

"Ah Watson, reducing your taxes was simplicity itself.
They were but elementary deductions."

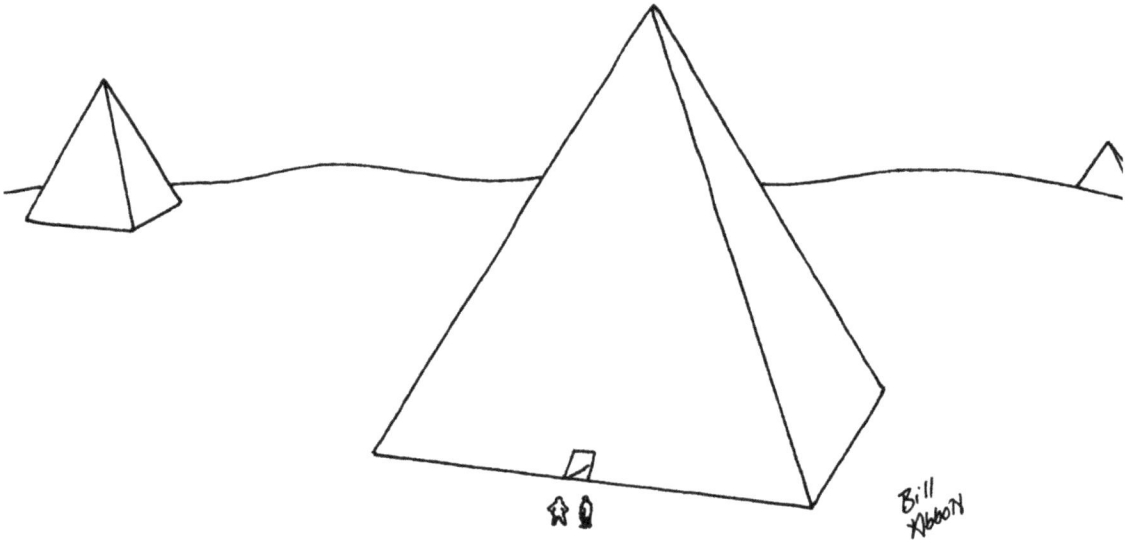

"Are your taxes based on usable living space or actual square footage?"

MASTERPIECES FROM THE GOLDEN AGE OF TAX-DEDUCTIBLE CONTRIBUTIONS

RHINESTONE ACCOUNTANT

Hey there, pretty lady! Got any numbers that need crunchin'?

"Actually, Harper, we don't see you as a partner. You've
been cast in more of character role."

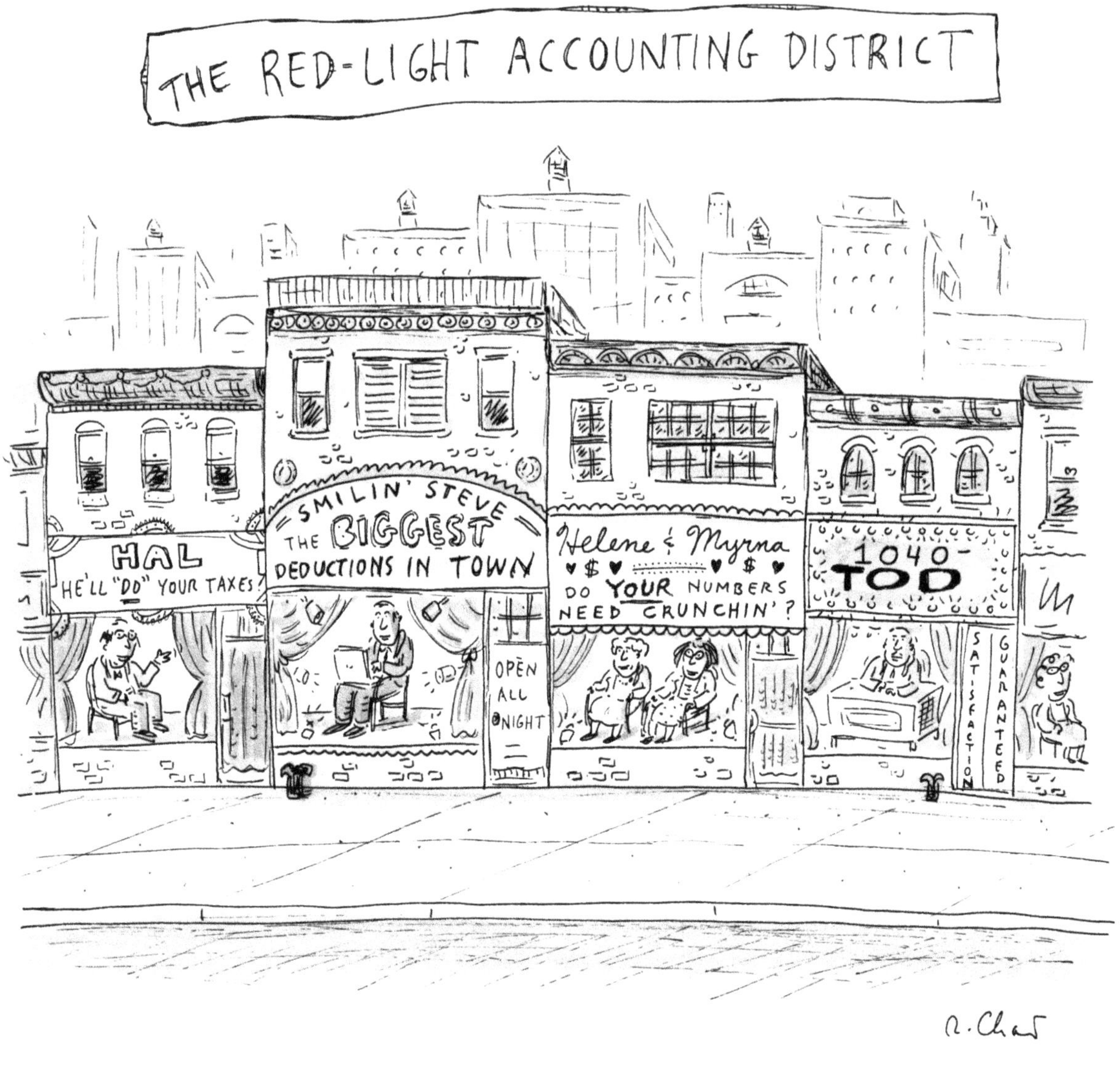
THE RED-LIGHT ACCOUNTING DISTRICT
HAL
HE'LL "DO" YOUR TAXES!
SMILIN' STEVE
THE BIGGEST
DEDUCTIONS IN TOWN
OPEN ALL NIGHT
Helene & Myrna
DO YOUR NUMBERS NEED CRUNCHIN'?
1040-TOD
SATISFACTION GUARANTEED

"We've agreed to count it as both a wave and a particle for tax purposes."

MANKOFF

I.R.S.

MERGER

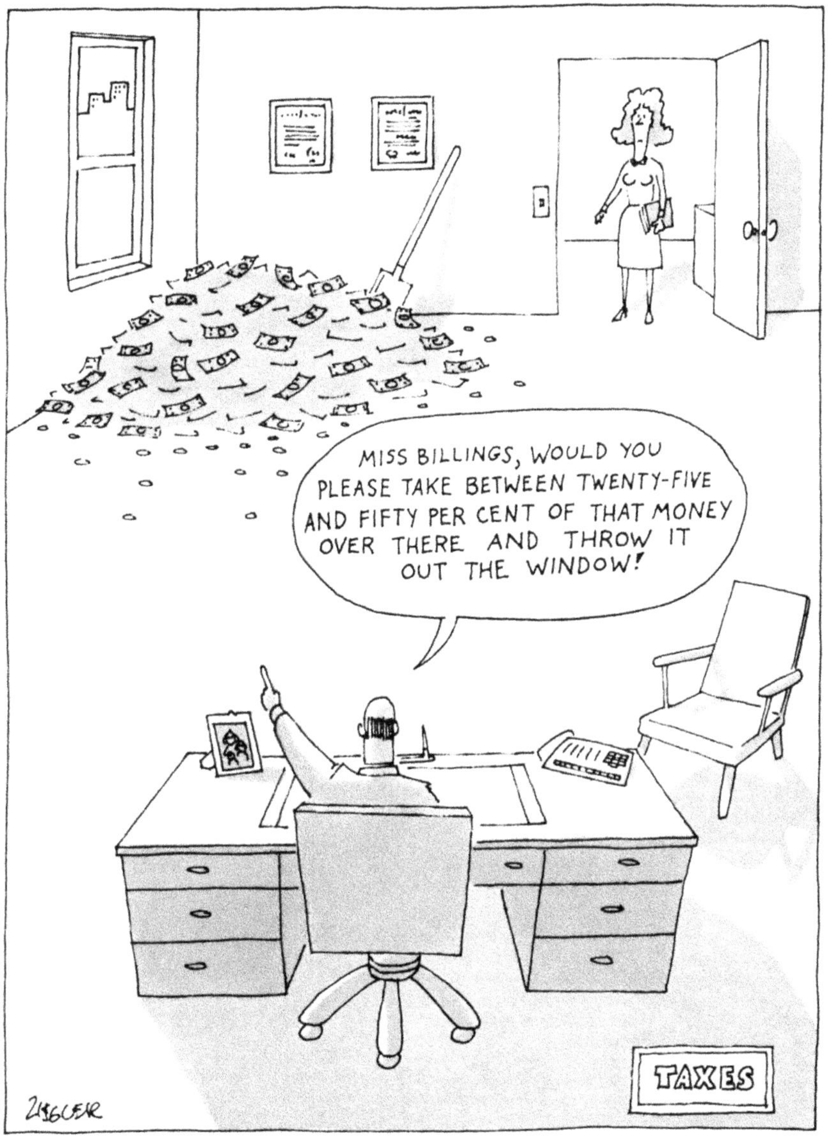
MISS BILLINGS, WOULD YOU PLEASE TAKE BETWEEN TWENTY-FIVE AND FIFTY PER CENT OF THAT MONEY OVER THERE AND THROW IT OUT THE WINDOW!
TAXES
ZIEGLER

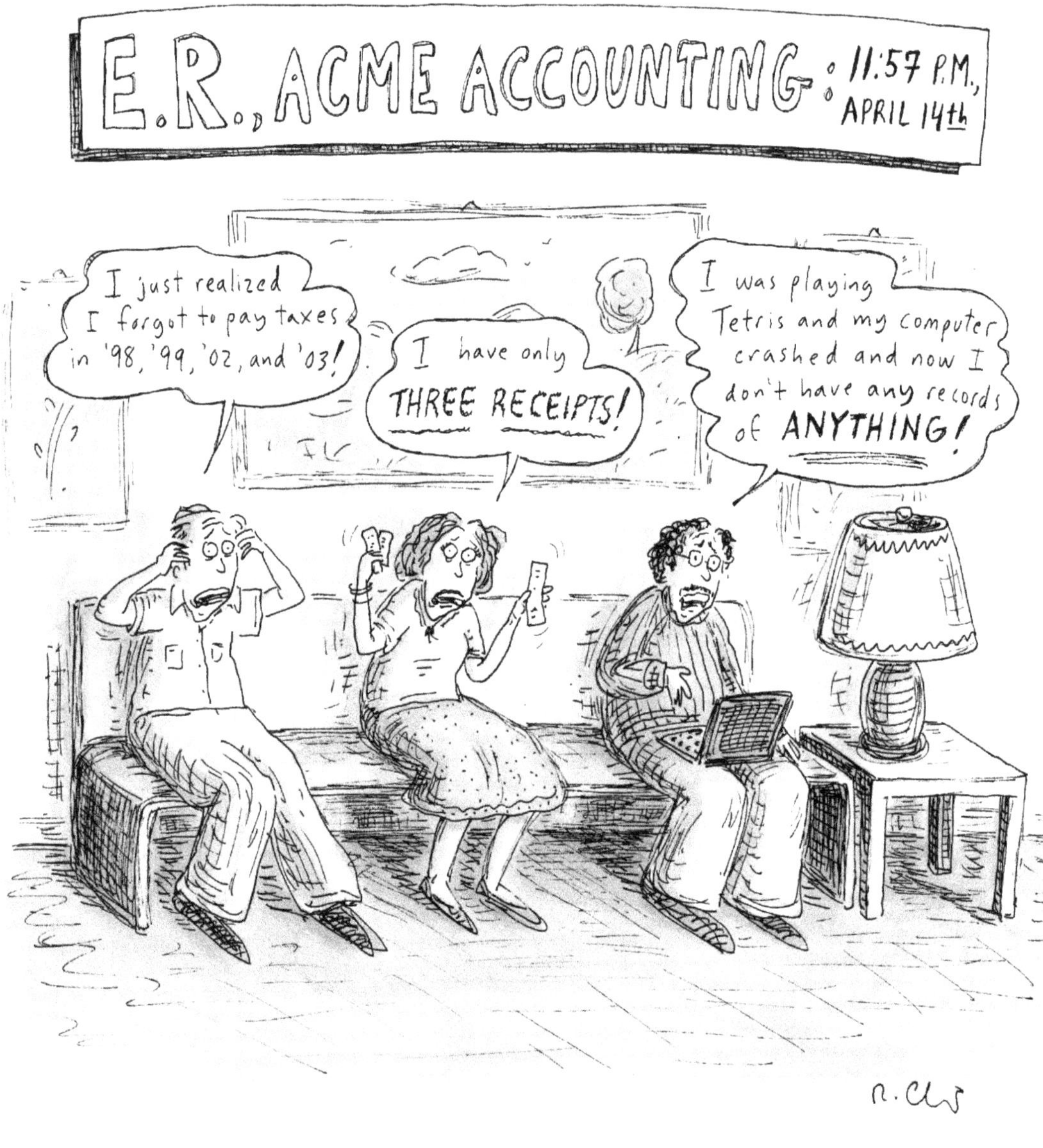
E.R., ACME ACCOUNTING: 11:57 P.M., APRIL 14th
I just realized I forgot to pay taxes in '98, '99, '02, and '03!
I have only THREE RECEIPTS!
I was playing Tetris and my computer crashed and now I don't have any records of ANYTHING!
R. Chast

NEW I.R.S. GUIDELINES

All bath toys are deductible.

Children with less than a B average are no longer deductible.

Mortgage payments made on houses not <u>completely</u> encased in aluminum siding are not deductible.

Three cats count as one dependent.

If somebody steps on your toe and then gives you $1.<u>00</u>, you must declare it.

I'm so sorry! Please accept this

For every glass of buttermilk consumed during the fiscal year, deduct $1.<u>50</u>.

R Chast

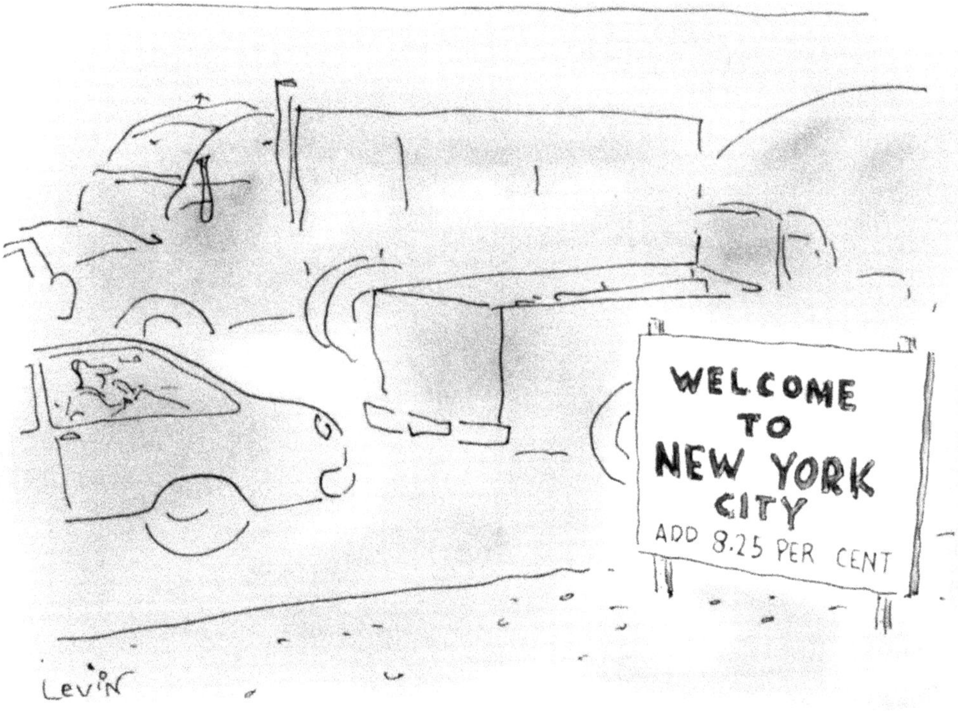
WELCOME
TO
NEW YORK
CITY
ADD 8.25 PER CENT
LEVIN

"*You know, the idea of taxation with representation doesn't appeal to me very much, either.*"

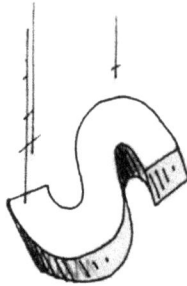

APRIL SHOWERS

"As far as I'm concerned, they can do what they want with the minimum wage, just as long as they keep their hands off the maximum wage."

"It was Socrates, wasn't it, who said, 'The unexamined life is not worth living'?"

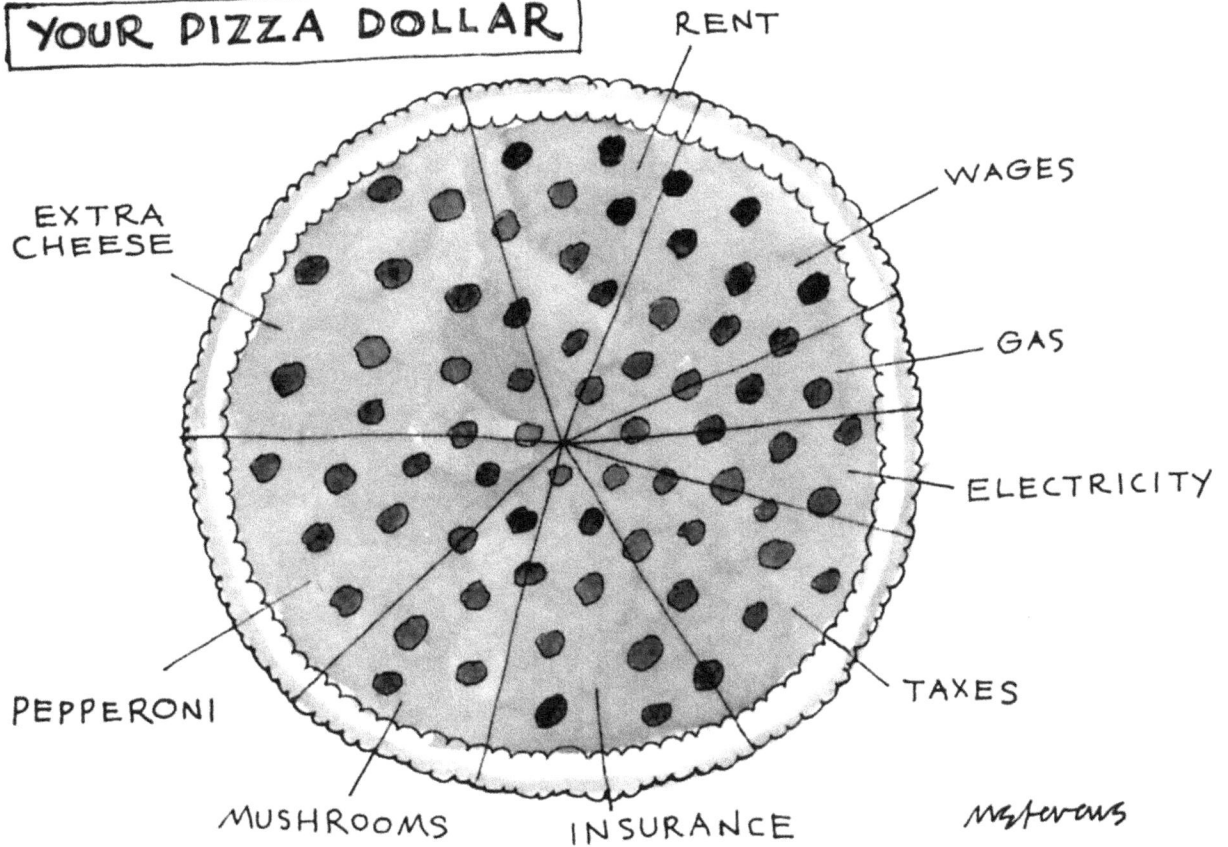

YOUR PIZZA DOLLAR

RENT

WAGES

GAS

ELECTRICITY

TAXES

INSURANCE

MUSHROOMS

PEPPERONI

EXTRA CHEESE

mstevens

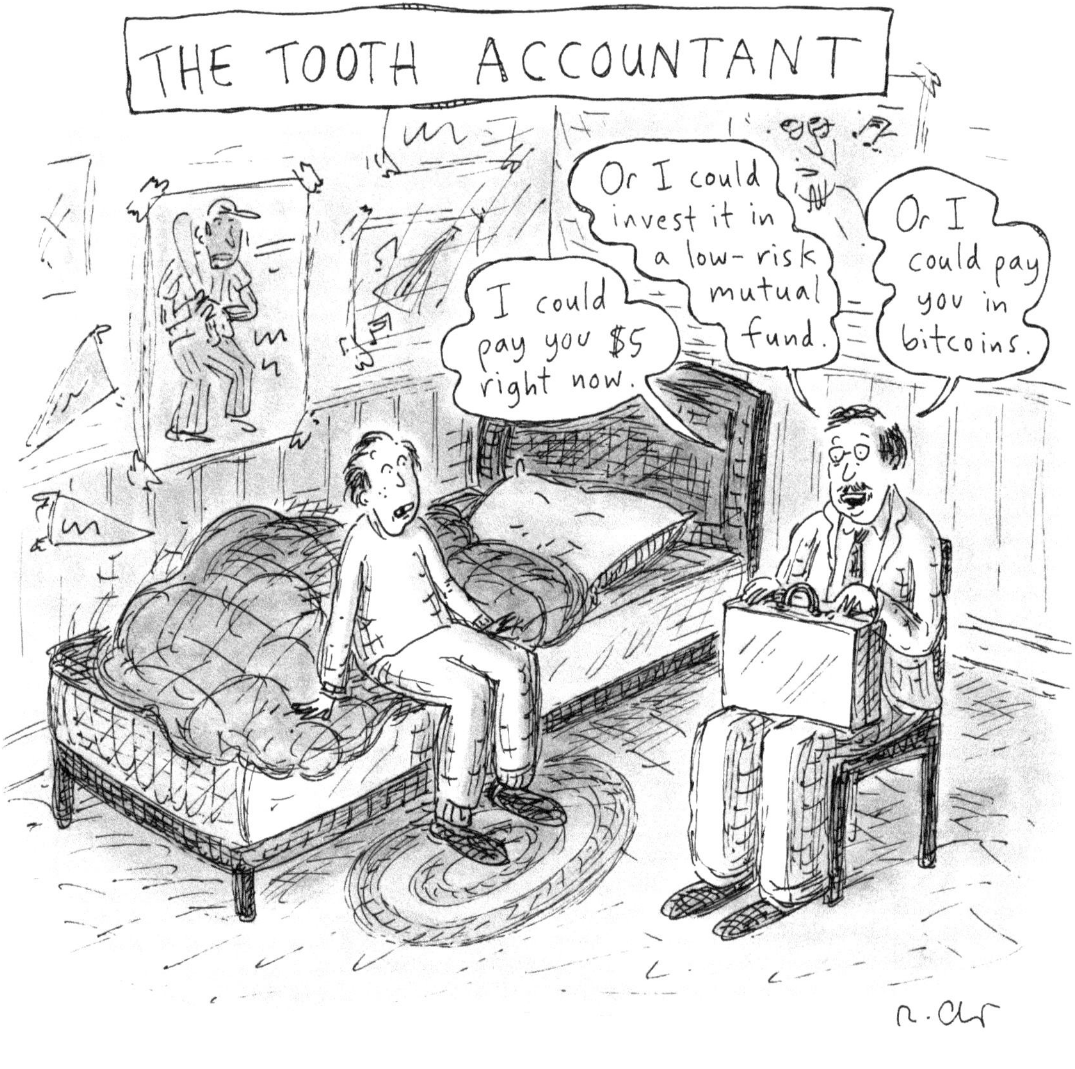
THE TOOTH ACCOUNTANT
I could pay you $5 right now.
Or I could invest it in a low-risk mutual fund.
Or I could pay you in bitcoins.
R. Chr

"New from accounting, sir. Two and two is four again."

"*Being an accountant gives him that extra aura of danger.*"

DAVE AND HIS COMMON-LAW ACCOUNTANT, PHIL

"I'm sick and tired of 'Generally Accepted Accounting Principles'."

"My job is in finance. This is just my hobby."

"Don't worry about a thing. Your taxes are too complicated for anyone to figure out."

"It's a dependent!"

"We've done what we can. Now it's all in the hands of the accountants."

"I'm a Schedule D kind of guy with a little Schedule E thrown in."

"You have to declare what you rob from the rich,
but you can deduct what you give to the poor."

"This is Fluffy, my pet money."

INTRODUCING...
THE 1040 - F.I.* FORM
* THE TAX RETURN FOR THE FINANCIALLY INCOMPETENT

① How much money do you guess you made last year?

☐ Under $10,000.

☐ Somewhere between $10,000 and $100,000.

☐ More than $100,000, but I don't know how or why.

② Did you save any receipts?

☐ I tried, but I just couldn't.

☐ I think there're some in a shoebox. I'll go look.

☐ No. What am I, an accountant?

③ Check payment preference.

☐ How could I owe anything? My year was lousy.

☐ Here's $15,000. If you need more, let me know.

☐ Blank check enclosed. You fill it in. Whatever.

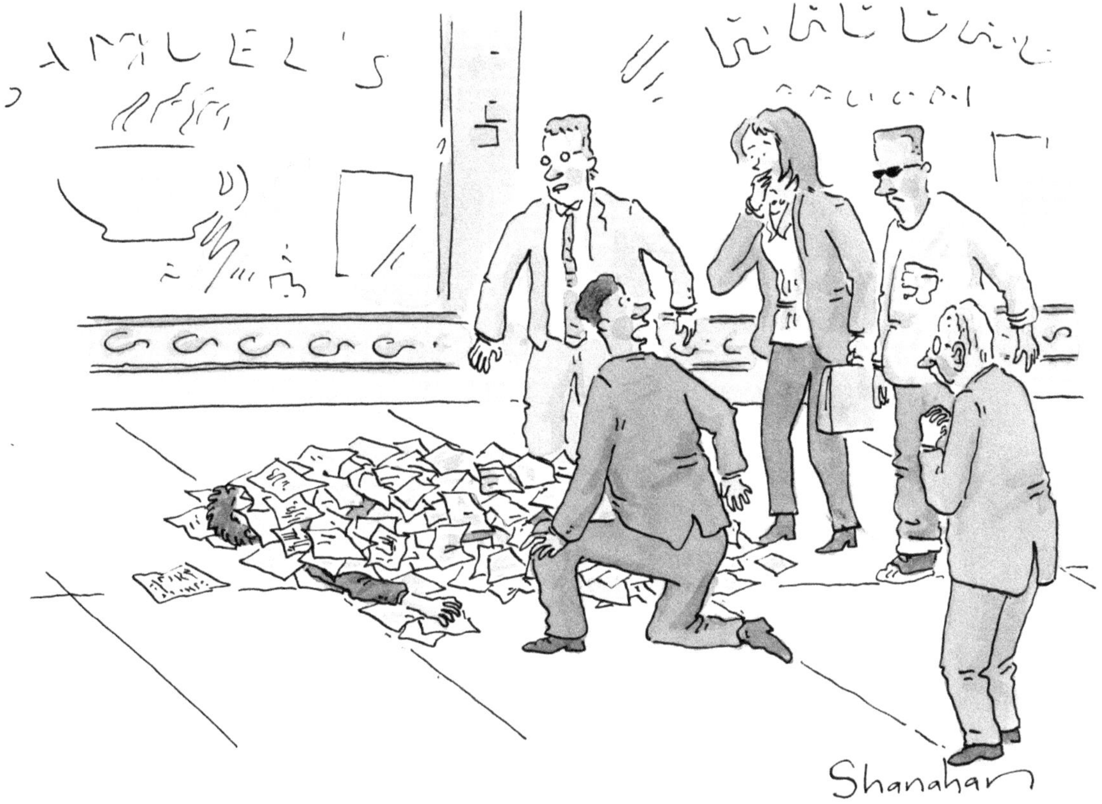
Shanahan

"Does anyone know C.P.A.?"

"We're trying to put the fun back into filing taxes."

APRIL
15 15 15 15 15
15 15 15 15 15 15 15
15 15 15 15 15 15 15
15 15 15 15 15 15 15
15 15 15 15

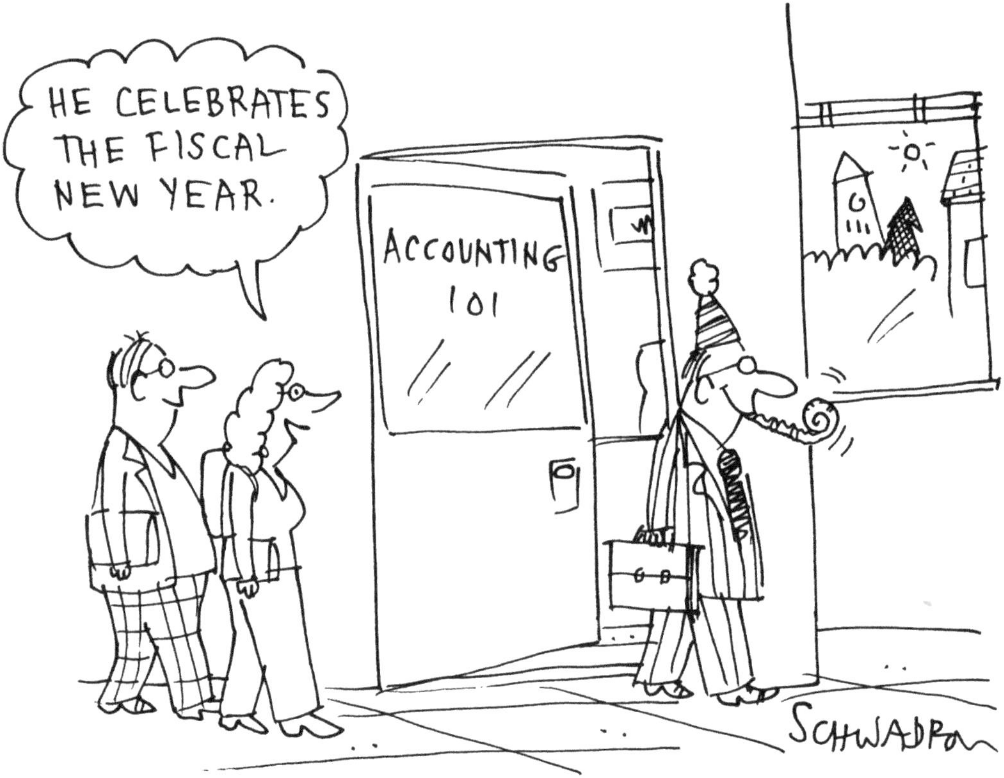
HE CELEBRATES THE FISCAL NEW YEAR.
ACCOUNTING 101
SCHWADRON

"I see you brought the pie charts."

"I've analyzed, condensed and simplified the data...it was a good quarter."

"*Daddy doesn't know any magic tricks. Daddy knows accounting tricks.*"

"*Oh, what the hell, I'll add another zero.*"

"It's the old story. I was in the middle of successful acting career when I was bitten by the accounting bug."

"We are neither hunters nor gatherers. We are accountants."

"I will grant you three wishes. You should know, however, that after taxes it will be reduced to one and a half wishes."

"Very creative, though it doesn't quite compare with what we're doing over in accounting."

"I don't see a way to balance the budget,
but I've discovered a way to win the lottery!"

"*And this is where the magic happens.*"

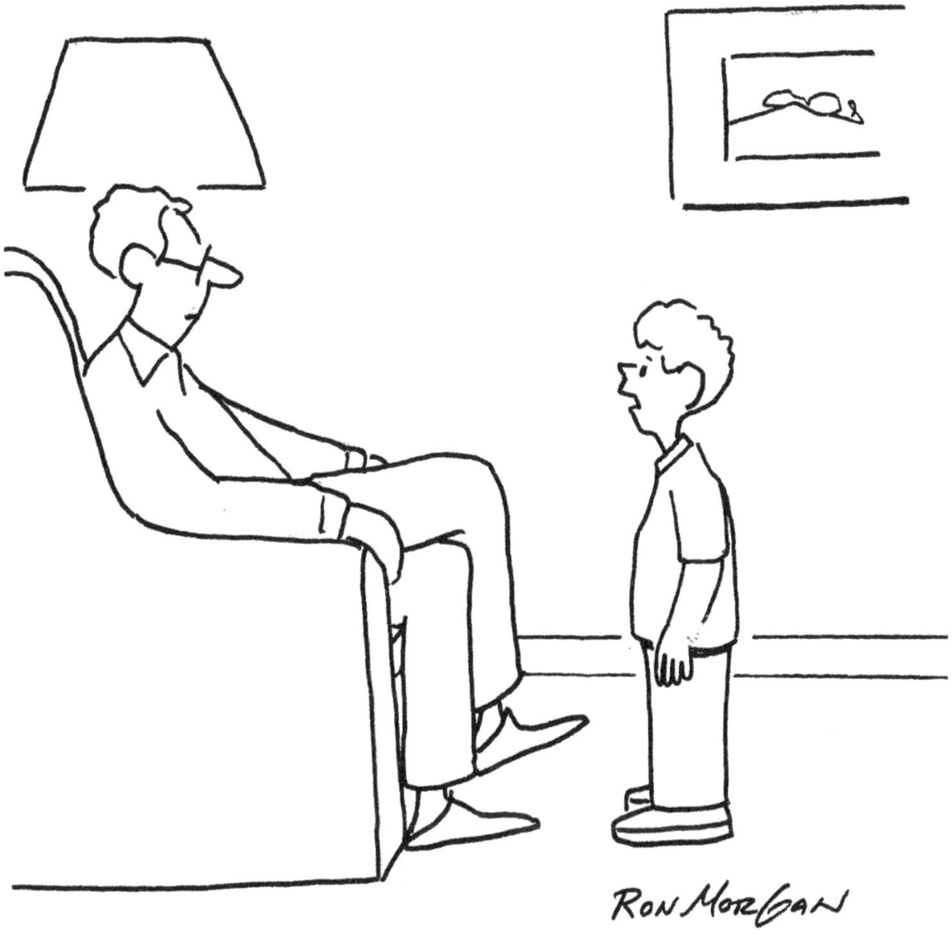
RON MORGAN

"You say you can't afford to raise my allowance -- could I please see the books?"

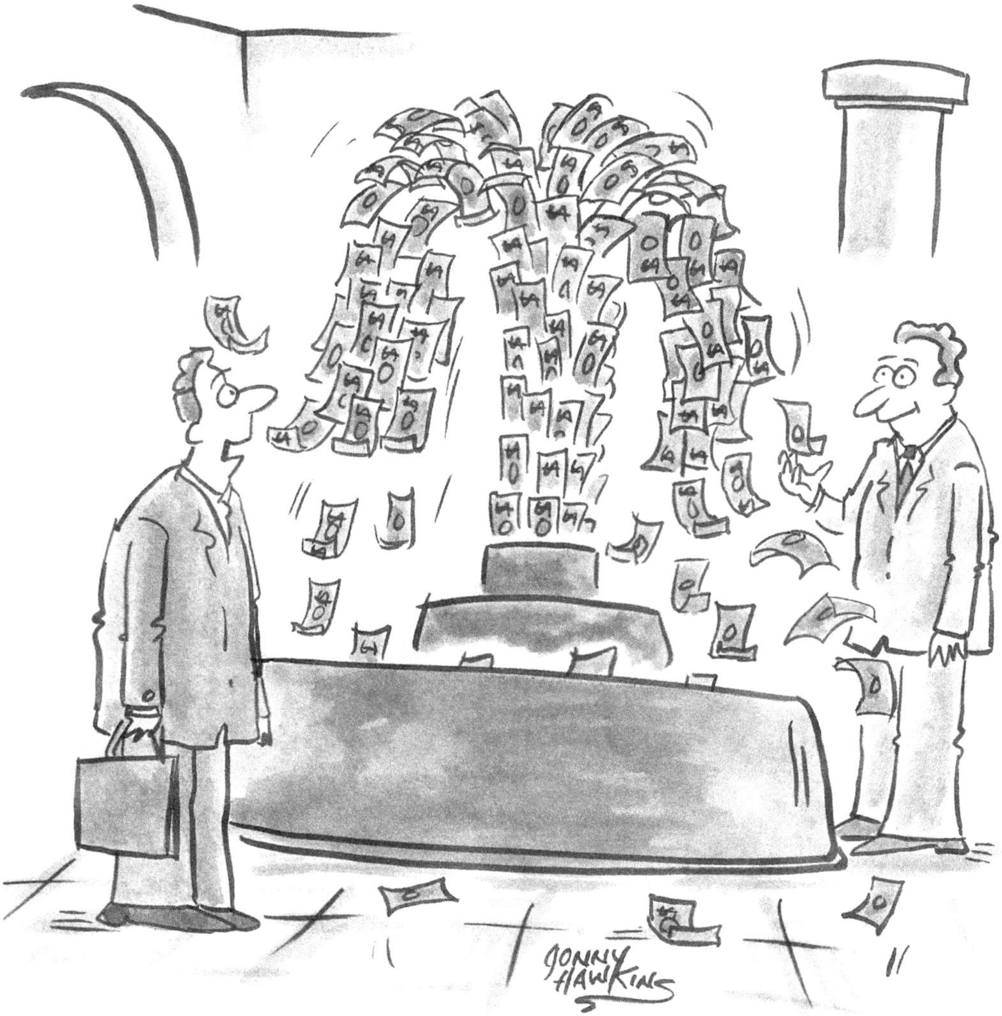
JONNY HAWKINS

"Great cash flow, Phil."

ACCOUNTING SCHOOL

"GO FORTH AND MULTIPLY, DIVIDE, ADD AND SUBTRACT."

"Don't be intimidated by his fifty million dollar salary...
Just think of his as a guy with a tax problem."

"*First the good news – we don't have to pay any corporate taxes this year.*"

"When I became known as 'The Accounting Wizard', the hat became inevitable."

"Our goal is to eliminate tax loopholes... so from now on they'll be called donut holes."

"Not only must I succeed, ... others must also pay my taxes."

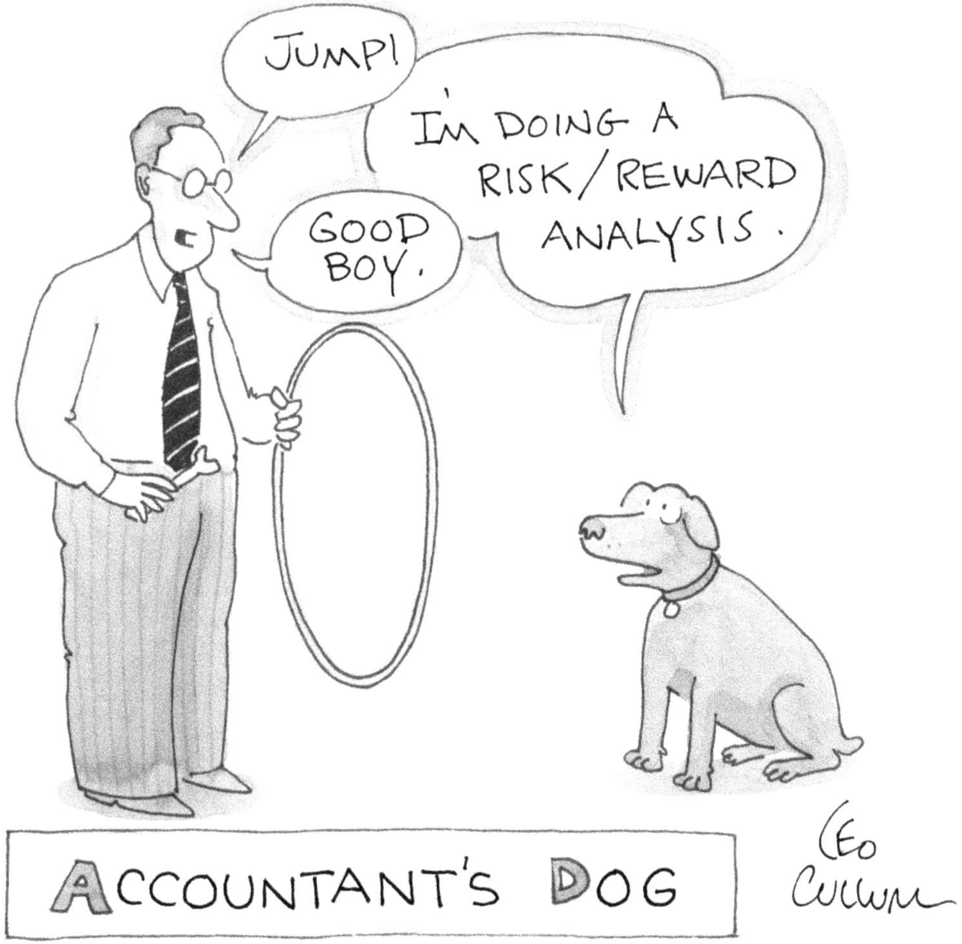
JUMP!
GOOD BOY.
I'M DOING A RISK/REWARD ANALYSIS.
ACCOUNTANT'S DOG

FORM 1040
SCHEDULE
"A"
LINE 15
GIFTS BY CASH
OR CHECK..

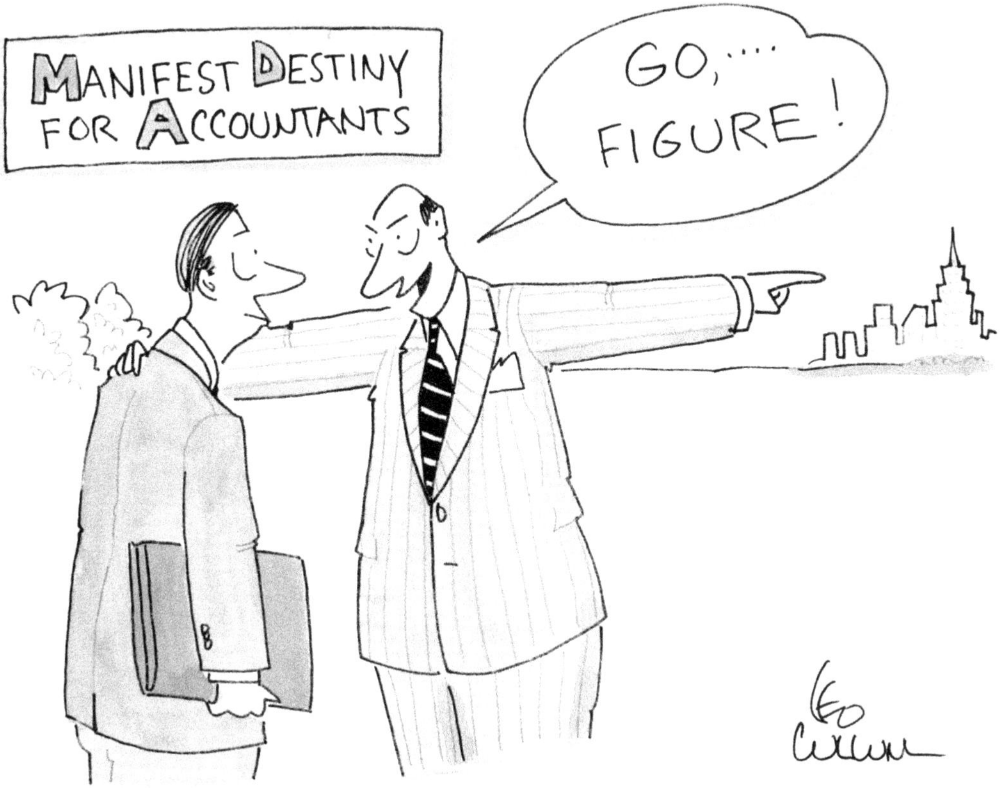
MANIFEST DESTINY
FOR ACCOUNTANTS
GO,....
FIGURE!

"I know you 'ran' the numbers but did you 'crunch' them?"

"I don't want to brag, but I have a loophole named after me."

"I'm a little concerned about my financial advisor.
He said to keep 60% in equities, 25% in bonds, and 25% in cash."

THE MEANING OF LIFE

TAX AVOIDANCE ADVICE

"This guy makes big money, but every penny goes to support his opulent life style. Let's give him a break."

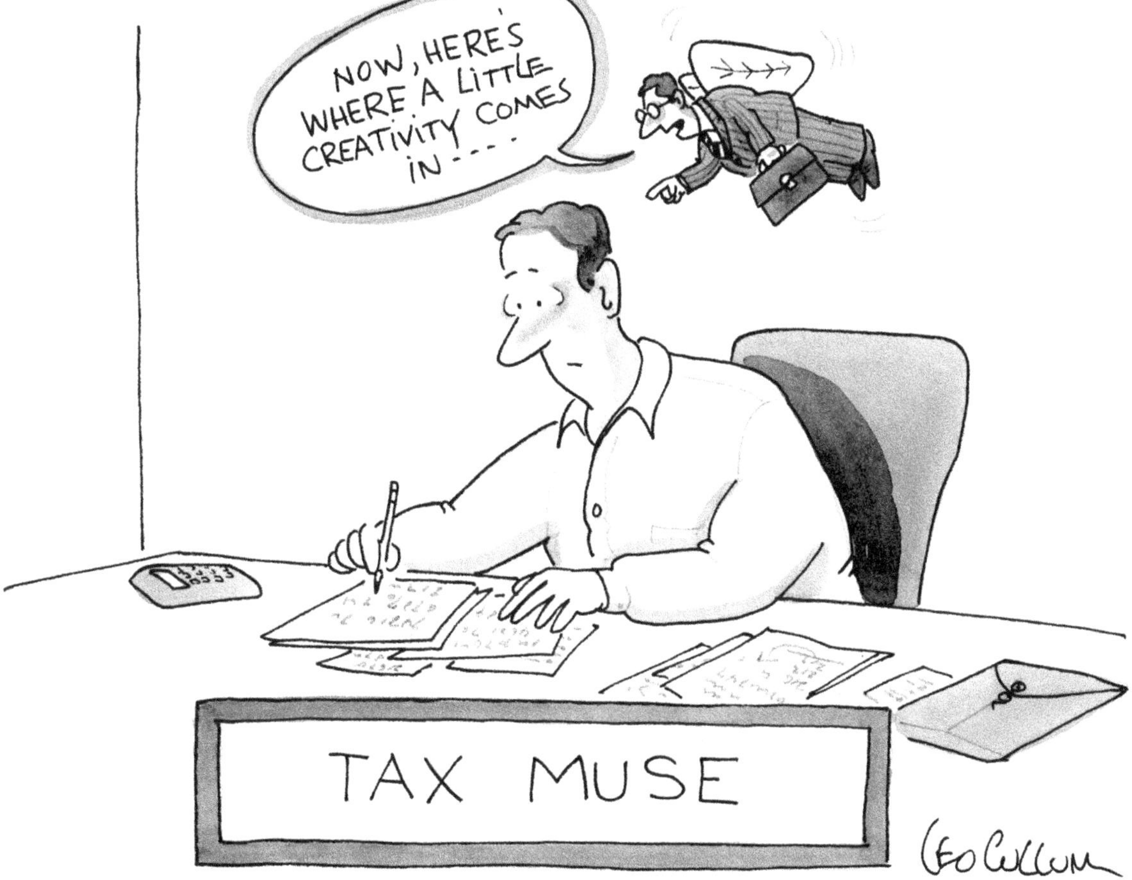
NOW, HERE'S WHERE A LITTLE CREATIVITY COMES IN----
TAX MUSE
LEO CULLUM

"My youngest is at the age when she can barely comprehend cost effective analysis."

"Trust me, son, if there was a monster under your bed I would have claimed it as a dependent by now."

Index of Artists

www.ingramcontent.com/pod-product-compliance
Lightning Source LLC
Chambersburg PA
CBHW040847100426
42813CB00015B/2732